CANADA
IN PICTURES:

VOLUME 3:
THE NORTHERN TERRITORIES

Dawson

Yukon

Whitehorse

Inuvik

Mackenzie
River

*Great
Bear
Lake*

Bank
Island

Victoria
Island

resolute

Baffin Island

Northwest
Territories

Nunavut

Gjoa
Haven

Iqalu

Yellowknife

Baker
Lake

Fort
Nelson

Great

First Edition, 2022

Published in Canada by Speedy Publishing Canada Limited Suite 3208 620 Nine Mile Dr Suite, Bedford, Nova Scotia B4A 0H4.

© 2022 Tripping Out, an Imprint of Speedy Publishing Canada Limited

Tripping Out are available at special discounts when purchased in bulk for industrial and sales-promotional use. For details contact our Speedy Publishing Canada Limited Suite 3208 620 Nine Mile Dr Suite, Bedford, Nova Scotia B4A 0H4.
Telephone (902) 442-8966
Fax: (902) 418-5362.
Email: help@speedypublishing.ca

Print Edition: 9780228236221
Digital Edition: 9780228236238
Hardcover Edition: 9780228236245

www.canadainpictures.ca

CONTENTS

YUKON TERRITORY
THE NORTHWEST TERRITORIES

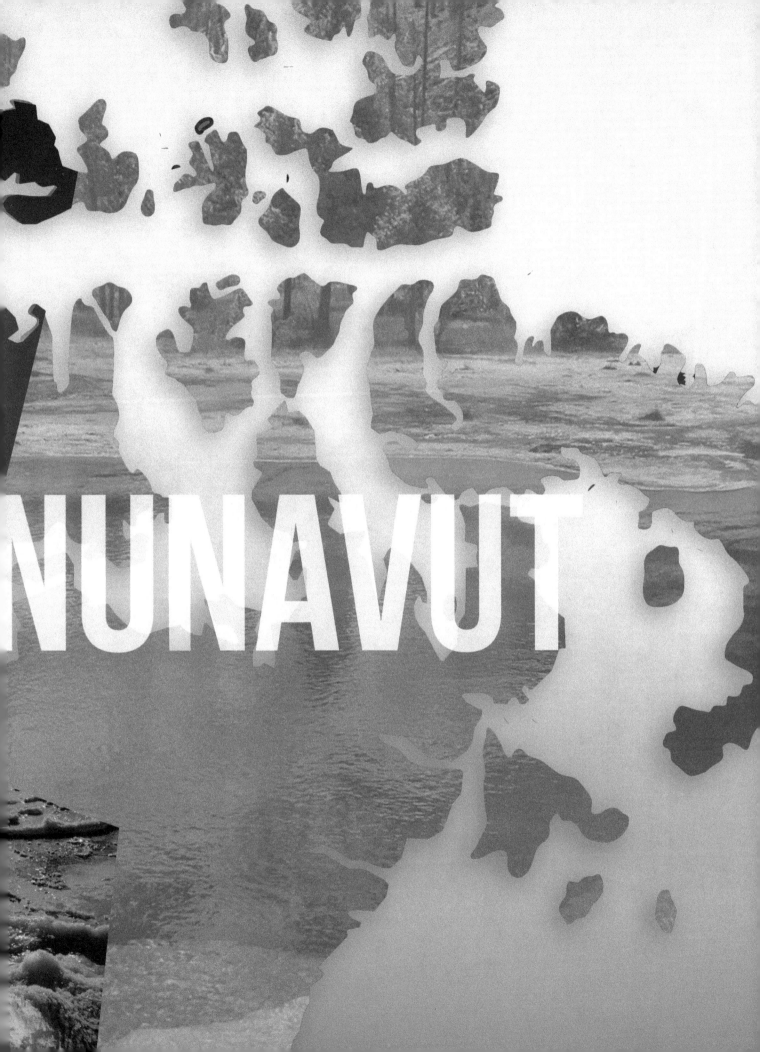

NUNAVUT

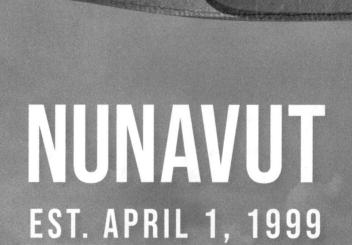

"OUR STRENGTH"

NUNAVUT

EST. APRIL 1, 1999

FACTS ABOUT THE PROVINCE

In the Inuktitut Inuit language, 'Nunavut' means 'our land'.

Nunavut is Canada's third territory, and the largest in the country as well. It encompasses about one-fifth of Canada's total land area.

It forms most of the Canadian Arctic Archipelago. Its islands have expanses of tundra, craggy mountains, and remote villages, which are only accessible by plane or boat.

The area is known for its indigenous Inuit people's artwork, carvings and handmade clothing. Inuit art is displayed at the Nunatta Sunakkutaangit Museum in Iqaluit, the territory's capital, located on Baffin Island.

The most common languages spoken in Nunavut are French, English, and Inuktitut.

FAMOUS PERSON BORN IN NUNAVUT

WHERE IN CANADA IS NUNAVUT?

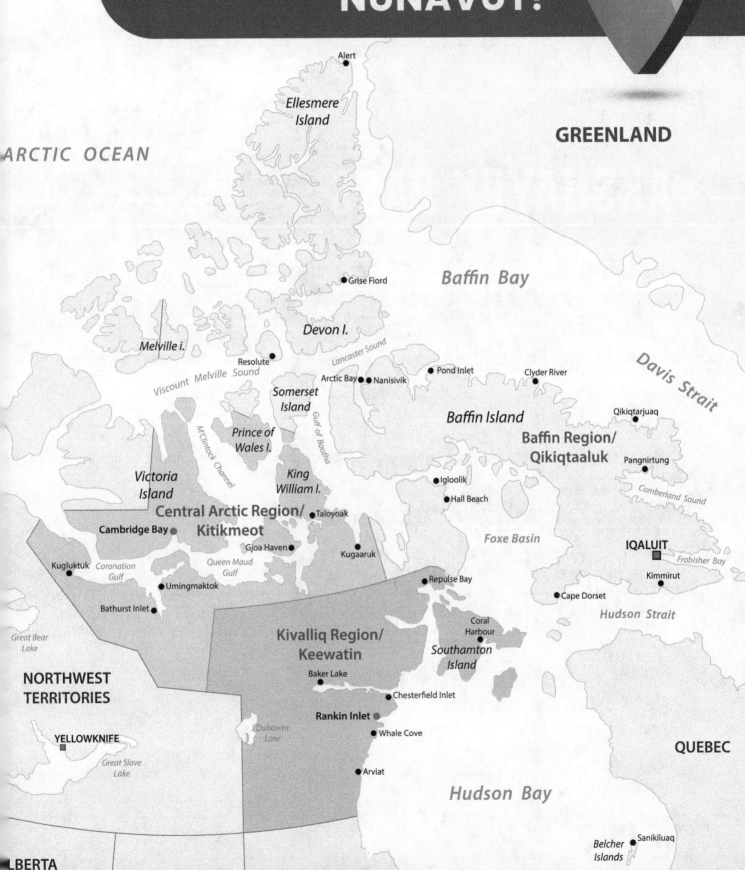

ARCTIC OCEAN

GREENLAND

Alert

Ellesmere Island

Baffin Bay

Melville i.

Grise Fiord

Devon I.

Davis Strait

Resolute

Viscount Melville Sound

Lancaster Sound

Pond Inlet

Clyder River

Arctic Bay ● Nanisivik

Somerset Island

Qikiqtarjuaq

M'Clintock Channel

Prince of Wales I.

Gulf of Boothia

Baffin Island

Baffin Region/ Qikiqtaaluk

Pangnirtung

Victoria Island

King William I.

Cumberland Sound

Central Arctic Region/ Kitikmeot

Igloolik

Cambridge Bay ●

Taloyoak

Hall Beach

Gjoa Haven ●

Kugaaruk

Foxe Basin

IQALUIT

Kugluktuk

Coronation Gulf

Queen Maud Gulf

Frobisher Bay

Kimmirut

Umingmaktok

Repulse Bay

Cape Dorset

Bathurst Inlet

Coral Harbour

Hudson Strait

Great Bear Lake

Kivalliq Region/ Keewatin

Southamton Island

NORTHWEST TERRITORIES

Baker Lake

Chesterfield Inlet

Dubawnt Lake

Rankin Inlet ●

YELLOWKNIFE

Whale Cove

QUEBEC

Great Slave Lake

Arviat

Hudson Bay

LBERTA

Belcher Islands

Sanikiluaq

SASKATCHEWAN

MANITOBA

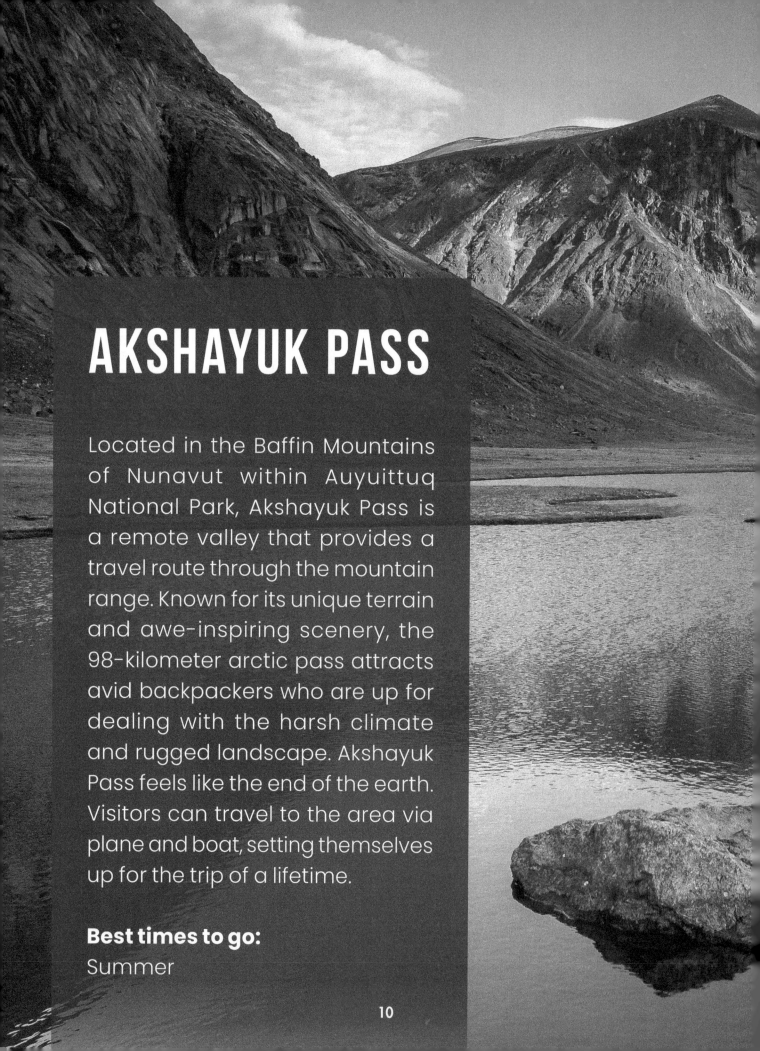

AKSHAYUK PASS

Located in the Baffin Mountains of Nunavut within Auyuittuq National Park, Akshayuk Pass is a remote valley that provides a travel route through the mountain range. Known for its unique terrain and awe-inspiring scenery, the 98-kilometer arctic pass attracts avid backpackers who are up for dealing with the harsh climate and rugged landscape. Akshayuk Pass feels like the end of the earth. Visitors can travel to the area via plane and boat, setting themselves up for the trip of a lifetime.

Best times to go:
Summer

Akshayuk Pass, Baffin Island, Nunavut

UKKUSIKSALIK NATIONAL PARK

Ukkusiksalik National Park is situated on the Nunavut mainland along the northernmost coast of Hudson Bay. The park offers visitors the opportunity to hike, boat and snowmobile in one of Canada's most beautiful and remote locations. It also features numerous prehistoric and European archaeological sites. A range of accommodations can be found in Baker Lake, Chesterfield Inlet, Naujaat and other nearby communities. The Ukkusiksalik National Park is easily reached by land or chartered plane.

Best times to go:
All Year

13

MOUNT ODIN

Located just south of Mount Asgard and on Baffin Island, Mount Odin is one of the highest points in Canada. Known for also being one of the top 10 highest points located in the eastern half of North America, the mountain rises over 7,000 feet. Climbing up can be a bit of a challenge as it's often covered in snow. There are areas that offer exceptional skiing conditions, which is one of the reasons why it's so popular among residents and tourists.

Best times to go:
Summer, Winter

OVAYOK TERRITORIAL PARK

Located about 15 kilometers east of Cambridge Bay on Victoria Island, a legendary mountain called Ovayok has been an important landmark for the Inuit people since ancient times. The 200-meter-high mountain served as a gathering place as the Inuit migrated annually inland from the sea ice. Today, Ovayok Territorial Park has five trails for hiking and camping. Ovayok is part of the Nunavut Territory, accessible only by sea and air. You're likely to see a herd of muskoxen grazing, and it's a worldwide destination for birdwatching.

Best times to go:
Spring, Summer

An ancient Inuit Inukshuk landmark, Qikiqtarjuaq, Broughton Island, Nunavut

ARVIA'JUAQ AND QIKIQTAARJUK NATIONAL HISTORIC SITE

Located in the Hudson Bay in Nunavut, Arvia'juaq and Qikiqtaarjuk National Historic Site is made up of two areas that have been inhabited by generations of Paallirmiut Inuit. These indigenous people used the land as summer camps, while taking advantage of its abundant natural resources. Known for the caribou herd migrations in May, this area is most accessible by snowmobile and ATV.

Best times to go:
Late Spring, Early Summer

SAINT JUDE'S ANGLICAN CATHEDRAL

Colloquially referred to as "Igloo Cathedral" because of its distinctive shape, Saint Jude's Anglican Cathedral is located in the heart of Iqaluit, Nunavut. As the official seat of the Diocese of The Arctic, Saint Jude's covers a larger district than any other Anglican diocese on Earth. After you visit the church to marvel at the details of the interior, feel free to visit Quammaarviit Territorial Park, take a hiking tour around Iqaluit, and reserve a day for snowmobiling if you're visiting in winter!

Best times to go:
Summer, Fall, Winter

CROKER BAY

Located along the southern coastline of Devon Island in Nunavut, Croker Bay is part of Lancaster Sound as well as a component of the Barrow Strait. Known for some of the largest glaciers in the Arctic, there are trails that you can follow that lead around the base of the glacier. Boat excursions are often taken in the bay to view the ice caps and the cliffs. This is an area that has started shrinking in size due to warmer temperatures.

Best times to go:
Spring, Summer, Winter

Croker Bay Glacier, in the Canadian Arctic, Nunavut

TUKTUT NOGAIT NATIONAL PARK

Visitors with the fortitude to make the long journey to Tuktut Nogait National Park will discover a wealth of natural beauty and an abundance of wildlife that's difficult to match. This remote park is located along Canada's northern coast near the border between Nunavut and the Northwest Territories. In addition to its other assets, the site also boasts a number of archaeological features that are sure to appeal to individuals with an interest in the history of northern Canada.

Best times to go:
Summer

The Hamlet of Paulatuk, home of the Inuvialuit and is the gateway community for Tuktut Nogait National Park, Nunavut

Akshayuk Pass, Auyuittuq National Park, Nunavut

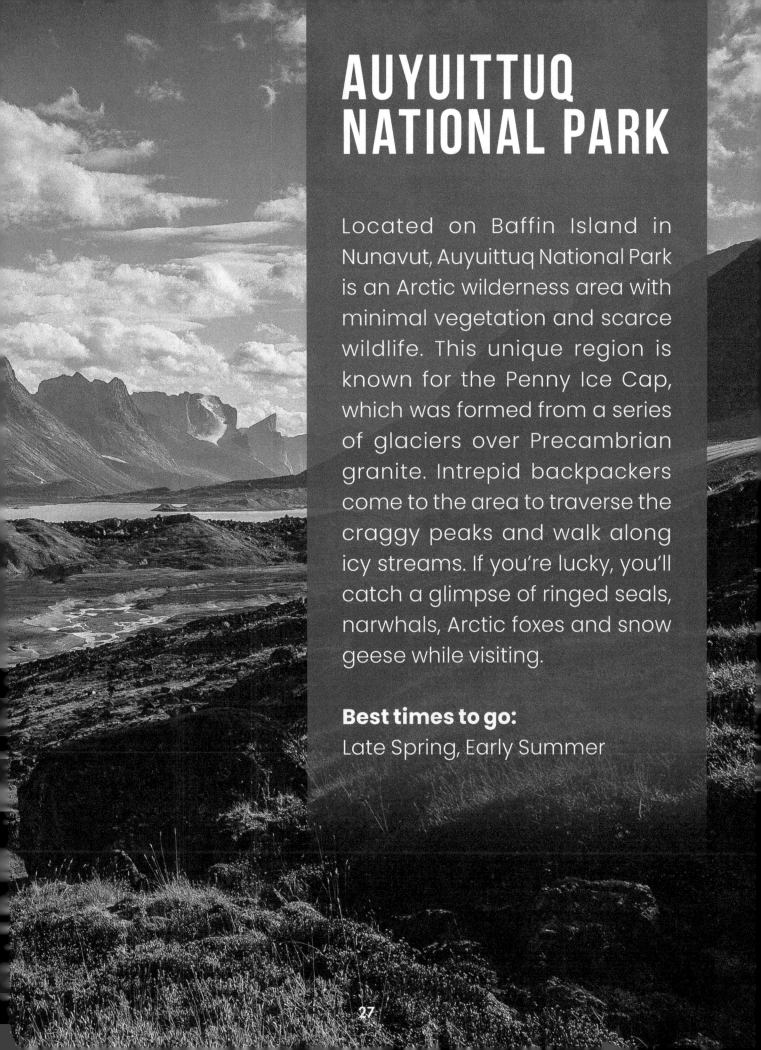

AUYUITTUQ NATIONAL PARK

Located on Baffin Island in Nunavut, Auyuittuq National Park is an Arctic wilderness area with minimal vegetation and scarce wildlife. This unique region is known for the Penny Ice Cap, which was formed from a series of glaciers over Precambrian granite. Intrepid backpackers come to the area to traverse the craggy peaks and walk along icy streams. If you're lucky, you'll catch a glimpse of ringed seals, narwhals, Arctic foxes and snow geese while visiting.

Best times to go:
Late Spring, Early Summer

Northern lights in Iqaluit, Nunavut

IQALUIT

Located in Nunavut, Iqaluit is the only city in the territory. It functions as the capital of Nunavut and is the largest community in the area. Iqaluit has been a traditional Inuit fishing hub for centuries. Although it is located below the Arctic Circle, its polar climate makes it a perfect location for participating in winter sports. An arena was built in 2002 to house the Arctic Winter Games. Visitors can learn more about the Inuit culture, marvel at the distinctive architecture and experience the natural beauty of the area.

Best times to go:
Spring, Summer, Fall

Evening light on Mount Thor in Auyuittuq National Park, Nunavut

MOUNT THOR

Located in the Baffin Mountains in Auyuittuq National Park, Nunavut, Mount Thor is a popular rock climbing and camping destination. The ecological wonder was named after the Norse god of thunder and is often referred to as Thor Peak. Known for the world's longest vertical drop, Mount Thor offers a challenging and jaw-dropping overhang. This is an excellent place to try paragliding or parachuting. Other visitors can stay on land, hiking and taking in the spectacular vistas.

Best times to go:
Summer

ELLESMERE ISLAND

Located within the Arctic Archipelago in Nunavut, Ellesmere Island is Canada's northernmost point of land and one of the coldest permanently inhabited places in the world. It is home to three settlements and has a population of less than 200 people. About 20% of the island is a protected national park. The area is rich in well-preserved fossils that tell us a great deal about the history of the Earth. Most people visit Ellesmere Island to see Arctic wildlife and hike through the breathtaking landscape.

Best times to go:
Summer

Hoodoos on Bylot Island, Sirmilik National Park, Nunavut

SIRMILIK NATIONAL PARK

Located within Northern Canada's Arctic Dorillera, Sirmilik National Park is home to Oliver Sound, the Borden Peninsula of Baffin Island, and vast stretches of Inuit-owned land. Named after the Inuit phrase for "place of glaciers," the park contains several ice caps, polar bears, and species of marine wildlife. Enjoy a "frozen safari" tour of the park's scenic tundra, traverse frigid waterways with the help of a friendly guide, and hike across Sirmilik's snowy fields!

Best times to go:
Spring, Fall, Winter

RANKIN INLET

Located on the Kudlulik Peninsula, Rankin Inlet is considered the largest hamlet in Nunavut. Known for being home to the only Inuit ceramics producer in the world, the inlet is also the second-largest settlement in Nunavut. Artists typically set up their work ranging from prints and castings to carvings and ceramics. There is a combination of flat areas with walking trails and rock formations that blend with the pieces of art that are shown at many of the shows that are held at Rankin Inlet.

Best times to go:
Spring, Summer, Fall

Inuksuk landmark in Rankin Inlet, Nunavut

BEECHEY ISLAND

Located in the heart of Nunavut's Wellington Channel, Beechey Island has been a National Historic Site of Canada since 1993. Although the island is primarily known for being an early step on famous Norweigan explorer Roald Amundsen's journey through the Northwest Passage, it is actually named after English portrait painter William Beechey. Make sure to visit each of the island's five archaeological sites, the historic Northumberland House, and explore the shipwrecked HMS Breadalbane!

Best times to go:
Spring, Summer, Fall

MOUNT ASGARD

Located in Auyuittuq National Park and named after Norse mythology's realm of the gods, Mount Asgard is most famous for being featured in one of the earliest James Bond films. Since a group of mountaineers first reached the summit via Mount Asgard's South Peak in 1971, more than 10 additional routes to the top have been mapped out. Schedule a 15-day tour to give yourself plenty of time to enjoy the surroundings, take a relaxing walk around the Weasel River, and head to nearby Glacier Lakes for a special view!

Best times to go:
Spring, Summer, Fall

Two towers of Mount Asgard, Auyuittuq National Park, Nunavut

FROBISHER BAY

Situated on the southeastern region of Baffin Island, Frobisher Bay is a pristine body of water measuring approximately 135 miles long by up to 25 miles wide. Named after English explorer Sir Martin Frobisher, this bay became the first recorded site of the Church of England's Holy Communion services in North America during September of 1578. On Frobisher Bay, you can go kayaking in the summer, fishing in the spring, boating in the fall, and kite-skiing in the winter!

Best times to go:
Spring, Summer, Winter

Morning light in Frobisher Bay, Nunavut

Bylot Island, Northwest Passage, Nunavut

BYLOT ISLAND

Located just to the northeast of Baffin Island in Nunavut, Bylot Island is a bird sanctuary and conservation area. Known for its rocky coastline and icy, mountainous interior, the island was an important hunting and whaling area. Today, it is recognized for its abundance of wildlife. It's home to more than 50 bird species and is a summer location for up to 150 polar bears. Visitors flock to the area for outdoor adventures, tours and wildlife viewing.

Best times to go:
Spring, Summer, Fall

KEKERTEN HISTORIC PARK

Located on an uninhabited island in the Qikiqtaaluk Region of Nunavut, Kekerten Historic Park is a destination of national historic significance. Known as a former whaling station, the park features a walkway that leads visitors through various stations, the whaler's graveyard and lookout spots. Each element is marked by an informational display. Visitors can drop by the Visitors' Center, which doubles as a museum and library, or stop in the galleries, which feature local art and handiwork.

Best times to go:
Spring, Summer, Fall

Kekerten Island. Kekerten Historic Park, Nunavut

AXEL HEIBERG ISLAND

Located in the Qikiqtaaluk Region in Nunavut, Axel Heiberg Island is part of the Arctic Archipelago. The uninhabited area is known for its remarkable fossil forests, which were not discovered until 1985.The fossilized trees never petrified because they were covered in a thick layer of silt. Experts believe that the island's Lost Hammer Spring has a habitat similar to that of Mars. Few visitors, besides scientists and a handful of adventure-seekers, come to the area.

Best times to go:
Summer

First snow of the summer on Axel Heiberg Island in Canada's high Arctic, Nunavut

QUTTINIRPAAQ NATIONAL PARK

Located on Ellesmere Island in Nunavut, Quttinirpaaq National Park is the second-largest park in Canada. Its name means "top of the world" in Inuktitut, and the park is home to Barbeau Peak, the tallest mountain in Nunavut. The extreme polar landscape is marked by ice caps and arid conditions, and it attracts only about 50 visitors each year. Fort Conger was founded there as a settlement and Arctic exploration camp and is now a Federal Heritage Building.

Best times to go:
Summer

"LARGER THAN LIFE"

YUKON TERRITORY

EST. JUNE 13, 1898

FACTS ABOUT THE PROVINCE

The Yukon territory measures in at a whopping 483,450 km² (that's about the size of Spain) and is situated east of Alaska, between British Columbia and the Arctic Ocean. As of March 2018, there were 40,000 people living in the Yukon—of those, 30,000 calling the capital city of Whitehorse home. The other 10,000 residents just really like their peace and quiet. The Yukon is home to the toughest dog sled race on Earth, the Yukon Quest, spanning more than a thousand miles (1,600 km).

Measuring only one square mile, the Carcross desert in the Yukon is affectionately known as the smallest desert in the world—not to be confused with the smallest dessert in the world, which we believe is a miniature tart somewhere in France.

The name "Yukon" originated from the Gwich'in native word "Yuk-un-ah," meaning "Great River," referring to the Yukon River that flows across the territory, through Alaska and into the Bering Sea.

FAMOUS PERSON BORN IN YUKON TERRITORY
TAHMOH PENIKETT
- ACTOR

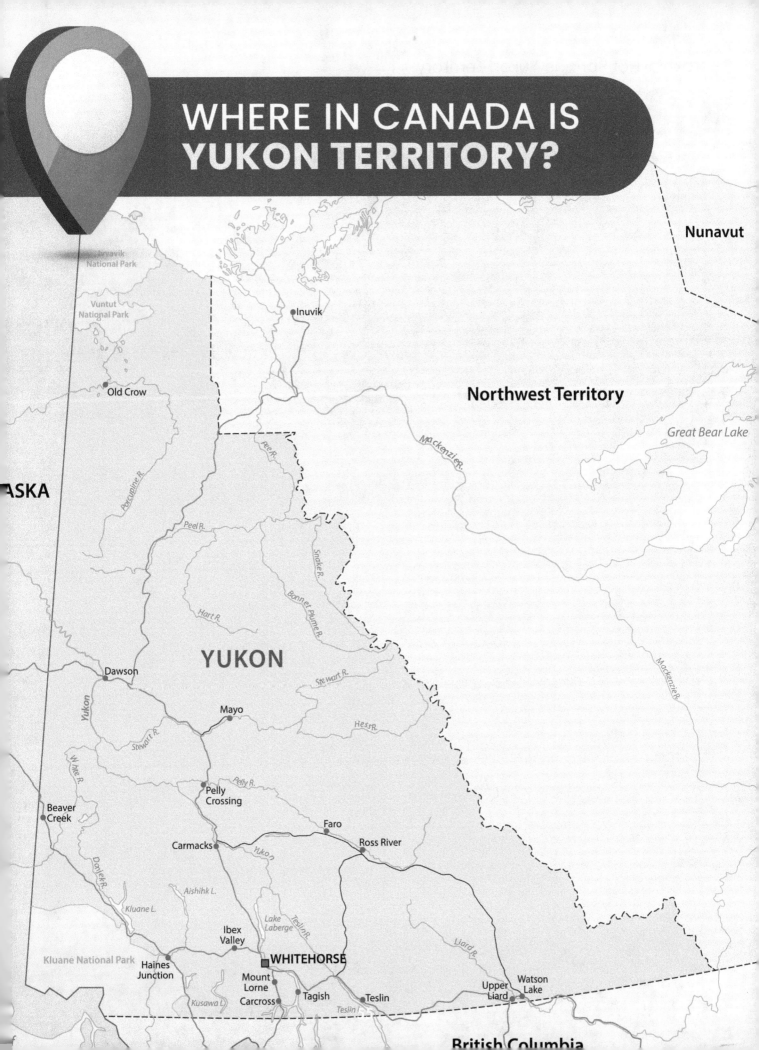

WHERE IN CANADA IS YUKON TERRITORY?

Nunavut

Ivvavik
National Park

Vuntut
National Park

Inuvik

Old Crow

ASKA

Northwest Territory

Great Bear Lake

Mackenzie R.

Peel R.

Porcupine R.

Peel R.

Snake R.

Bonnet Plume R.

Hart R.

YUKON

Stewart R.

Mackenzie R.

Dawson

Yukon R.

Mayo

Hess R.

Stewart R.

White R.

Pelly R.

Pelly
Crossing

Beaver
Creek

Faro

Carmacks

Yukon

Ross River

Donjek R.

Aishihk L.

Kluane L.

Liard R.

Lake
Laberge

Teslin R.

Ibex
Valley

Kluane National Park

WHITEHORSE

Haines
Junction

Mount
Lorne

Upper
Liard

Watson
Lake

Kusawa L.

Carcross

Tagish

Teslin

Teslin L.

British Columbia

Takhini Hot Springs, Yukon Territory

TAKHINI HOT SPRINGS

Sitting just outside the border of Whitehorse, Takhini Hot Springs is home to some of the Yukon's most expansive campgrounds. The grounds contain over 80 camping sites in total, and the hot springs have been operated by a local business for more than a century. Notably, the springs also contain a cooler pool that usually stays under 100 degrees Fahrenheit. Explore more than 300 acres of Canadian wilderness, book a dogsled tour in winter, and take part in the famous International Hair Freezing contest!

Best times to go:
Spring, Fall, Winter

FORT SELKIRK

Situated near the junction of the Pelly and Yukon Rivers in Central Yukon, Fort Selkirk is a former trading post and original home to the Selkirk First Nation, which relocated its inhabitants to Pelly Crossing, Yukon, following the construction of the Klondike Highway. It now boasts the Fort Selkirk Historic Site and Canada's northernmost volcanic field. This destination is accessible via plane or boat and offers no road access.

Best times to go:
Spring, Summer, Fall

Fort Selkirk Historic Site, Yukon Territory

MIDNIGHT DOME

Located near Yukon's Dawson City, the Midnight Dome is a beautiful mountain. It's known for its historical setting, hiking trails, and stunning views. Depending on your skill level, reach the summit with either moderate or strenuous routes. Once you're at the top, snap some photos! You'll see panoramic views of the Klondike Valleys and Yukon River. The Ogilvie Mountain Range is also visible. Next, pop over to Dawson City to learn about the Klondike Gold Rush.

Best times to go:
Summer

Midnight Dome above Dawson City overlooking the Yukon River, Yukon Territory

Autumn at the Yukon Wildlife Preserve, Yukon Territory

YUKON WILDLIFE PRESERVE

Located 25 minutes north of Whitehorse lies the 700-acre Yukon Wildlife Preserve. It offers some of the best wildlife viewing and photo opportunities in the world. You can observe 13 species of northern Canadian mammals in their native habitats. Walk, bike or even ski in winter on the 5-kilometer trail around the reserve. Or take the bus tour with one of their knowledgeable and friendly guides. Don't worry – they'll let you off the bus to take pictures and experience the wildlife up close.

Best times to go:
All Year

BENNETT BEACH

Nestled into the Yukon mountains, Bennett Beach is a hidden gem that offers activities such as fishing, sailing, swimming, and much more. During Canada's warmest months, you can find many locals flying kites and enjoying the soft, sandy shoreline. Even on the hottest days, you'll find the water's brisk temperatures to be quite refreshing. When you've had enough of the beach, go to the famous Emerald Lake, check out the Carcross Desert, and visit the Caribou Crossing Trading Post!

Best times to go:
Spring, Fall, Summer

Bennett Lake in Carcross, Yukon Territory

GREY MOUNTAIN

The Grey Mountain Trail, which is one of the Yukon's most famous hiking destinations, features three summits. Each summit's route has its own special characteristics, with thick vegetation and breathtaking views making frequent appearances. The trail stretches five kilometers in total, and most tourists are able to complete the trip to all three peaks in under seven hours. While you're in Whitehorse to hike Grey Mountain, make sure to visit the local glassblowing shop, look for caribou in the mountains, and take a canoe trip down the Yukon River!

Best times to go:
Summer. Fall, Winter

An aerial view of Chadburn Lake and Grey Mountain, Yukon Territory

Lapie Canyon, Yukon Territory

LAPIE CANYON

With 20 campsites, steep cliffs, and excellent rafting, Yukon's Lapie Canyon is a favorite of adventurers and casual tourists alike. Along Lapie Canyon's steep, graded walls, you can see ravens and other nesting birds building their homes. In addition, rare Yukon plants, such as the goldenweed, bloom across the campgrounds in the warmer months of the year. Tame the waters of the Lapie River with a canoe or a kayak, scale jagged ridges by foot to enjoy spectacular views, and cross the bridge over Pelly Barge if you dare!

Best times to go:
Spring, Summer, Fall

DAWSON CITY

Located at the confluence of the Yukon and Klondike Rivers, Dawson City, Yukon, is the second-largest city in the Yukon Territory. Dawson City was the center of the Yukon Gold Rush, and it grew to 40,000 residents nearly overnight. Today, visitors can experience one of the eight National Historic Sites that are located in the city, the most famous of which is the Dawson Historical Complex with its boom-town architecture.

Best times to go:
Spring, Summer, Fall

Main street with traditional wooden houses in Dawson City, Yukon Territory

Emerald Lake, Yoho National Park, Yukon Territory

EMERALD LAKE

Noted for its charming green water, Emerald Lake sits between mile 73 and mile 74 of the world-famous South Klondike Highway. The color of Emerald Lake's water results from a combination of the high amount of calcium carbonate coming in from a nearby mountain range and the limestone erosion of glaciers that filled the area more than 10,000 years ago. Visit the Takakkaw Falls, walk through the Spiral Tunnels at nearby Yoho National Park, and take a guided tour of the trilobite site at Mount Stephen.

Best times to go:
Spring, Summer

The Sign Post Forest in Watson Lake, Yukon Territory

SIGN POST FOREST

Located in Watson Lake, Yukon, Sign Post Forest is an enormous display of signed dinner plates, license plates, welcome signs, and street signs that people consider to be one of the most charming landmarks on the Alaska Highway. Sign Post Forest was originally started to help civil engineers learn the distances between various nearby points, but the area took on a life of its own when Pvt. Carl K. Lindley from the United States Army added a sign that pointed towards his hometown. After you've made your own contribution to the landmark, relax for a few hours at the Rancheria Falls Creation Site, pick up a souvenir from the Northern Beaver Post Gift Shop, and spend a while at the nearby Northern Lights Centre!

Best times to go:
Spring, Summer, Fall

TOMBSTONE TERRITORIAL PARK

Tombstone Territorial Park is located in the central area of the Yukon. Known for being the Patagonia of the country, the park offers beautiful views of the surrounding area for miles to see with hiking and camping being among the most popular activities. The park protects many of the permafrost areas in the country as well as several types of wildlife. Fall colors are stunning, and you can often view the northern lights with ease throughout the year.

Best times to go:
Spring, Fall, Winter

Footbridge over Miles Canyon, Yukon River near Whitehorse, Yukon Territory

MILES CANYON

Located a few kilometers from downtown Whitehorse, Yukon, Miles Canyon is a stunning gorge that was carved into prehistoric volcanic rock by the Yukon River. Known for its striking basalt cliffs, Miles Canyon attracts thousands of tourists each year. Its accessibility makes it an ideal recreation destination for people of all ages. Cross the suspension bridge across the rushing Yukon River, or do some sightseeing in the historic mining town. Hikers will enjoy the vast network of trails.

Best times to go:
Late Spring, Summer, Early Fall

KLUANE NATIONAL PARK AND RESERVE

Home to more than 15 of Canada's 20 tallest mountain peaks, Kluane National Park and Reserve is a UNESCO World Heritage Site that dominates the southwestern edge of the Yukon. In addition to its towering mountains, Kluane National Park And Reserve contains massive forests, titanic glaciers, and tons of charming spots to have a picnic! Take a rafting excursion down the Alsek River, fish for sockeye salmon, and try a hike up King's Throne Peak if you're up for a challenge.

Best times to go:
Spring, Summer, Fall

MOUNT LOGAN

Coming in second on the list of North America's highest peaks, Mount Logan can be found less than 30 miles away from the northern tip of the Yukon's border with Alaska. Amazingly, Mount Logan's height is still rising due to nearby tectonic activity. Even in the summer, the temperature anywhere on the mountain struggles to reach above zero degrees Fahrenheit. Enjoy a night of luxurious hospitality at the Mount Logan EcoLodge, try a partial climb with an international mountain guide, and take a rafting tour down the Dezadeash River.

Best times to go:
Spring, Summer

IVVAVIK NATIONAL PARK

Ivvavik National Park is located in the far northern reaches of Canada's Yukon and encompasses thousands of square kilometres of some of the most beautiful and untouched terrain in the country. An on-site base camp offers visitors the important amenities as well as a place to launch excursions into the park. Kayaking and rafting enthusiasts are sure to love the Firth River with its Class IV rapids while land-based explorers can take advantage of the park's numerous hiking trails.

Best times to go:
Summer

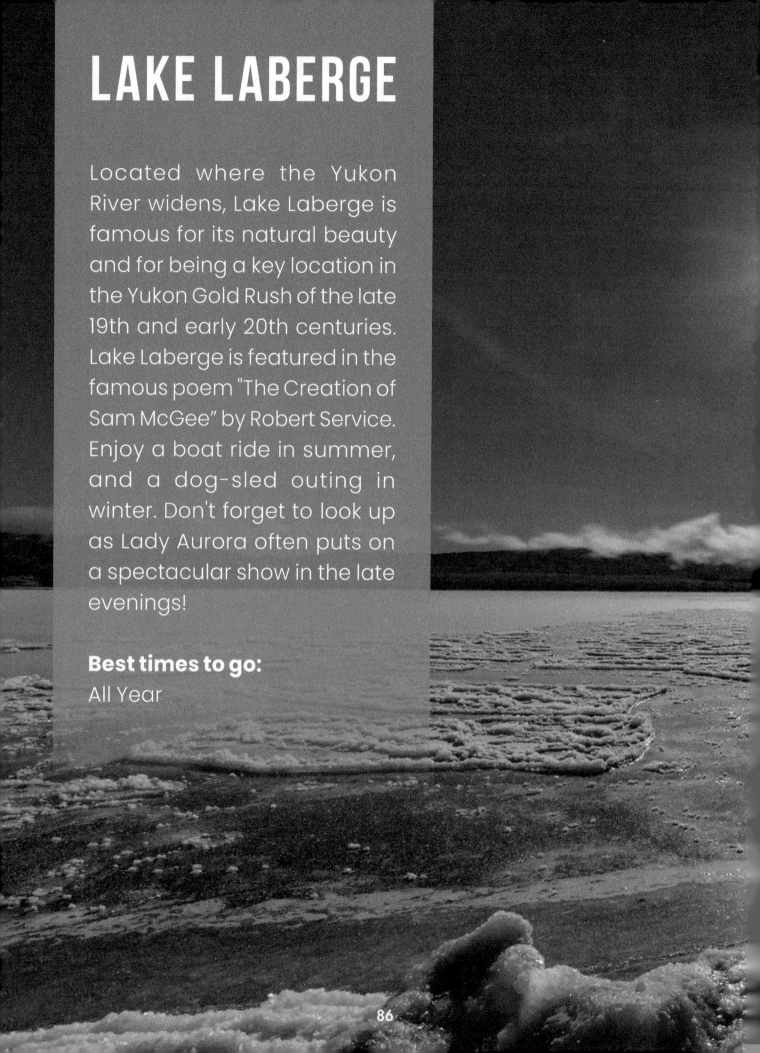

LAKE LABERGE

Located where the Yukon River widens, Lake Laberge is famous for its natural beauty and for being a key location in the Yukon Gold Rush of the late 19th and early 20th centuries. Lake Laberge is featured in the famous poem "The Creation of Sam McGee" by Robert Service. Enjoy a boat ride in summer, and a dog-sled outing in winter. Don't forget to look up as Lady Aurora often puts on a spectacular show in the late evenings!

Best times to go:
All Year

Frozen Lake Laberge, Yukon Territory

Carcross Desert, Yukon Territory

CARCROSS DESERT

Located near White Pass and believed to be the smallest desert in the world, Carcross Desert only takes up about one square mile. In reality, this "desert" is actually a small series of sand dunes that were formed from silt deposits during the Last Glacial Period over 11,000 years ago. The nearby mountains protect Carcross Desert from precipitation, creating an inviting habitat for several of Canada's rarest plants. Hit the dunes for a sandmobile adventure, make your way over to the historic Yukon Railway, and visit the spunky Skookum Jim House!

Best times to go:
Spring, Summer

KATHLEEN LAKE

Located in the southern area of Haines Junction and close to Kluane National Park, Kathleen Lake is a popular destination for those who enjoy outdoor recreational activities. Known for its exceptional hiking trails, you can enjoy a picnic at one of the tables, set sail on a boat, or cast your line to go fishing. Swimming is also a popular activity in the summer. Tent and RV camping are available, and the winter season offers cross-country skiing for those who want to do something a bit more challenging.

Best time to go:
Spring, Summer, Winter

Kathleen Lake, Yukon Territory

VUNTUT NATIONAL PARK

Located in Yukon, Canada, Vuntut National Park is an arctic treasure. It's known as the home of the Vuntut Gwitchin First Nation people. This area is remote, so your best bet is to fly into the nearby town of Old Crow. The park doesn't have any facility or developed trails, so it's perfect for experienced adventurers. Make detailed plans before backpacking through the sparkling wilderness! In the spring, you can watch Porcupine Caribou migrate across the land.

Best times to go:
Spring, Summer

Arctic Tundra, British Mountains, Vuntut National Park, Yukon Territory

DEZADEASH LAKE

Once the site of a military camp during World War II, Dezadeash Lake borders the Saint Elias Mountains and Kluane National Park. The aforementioned military camp has since been converted to what is now known as Dezadeash Lodge. Trout find the lake's oxygen-rich water to be an inviting habitat, making Dezadeash Lake the perfect place to spend an afternoon fishing. Take advantage of the nearby campgrounds, grab a filling lunch at the Mile 1016 Pub, and hike Rock Glacier Trail.

Best times to go:
Spring, Summer, Fall

FIVE FINGER RAPIDS

Featured in the famous Alastair Humphrey novel Thunder and Sunshine and in Jack London's The Call of the Wild, the Five Finger Rapids are located less than 25 kilometers to the north of Carmacks on the Yukon River. Each of the "fingers" is a narrow water channel, and a series of four islands in the middle produces a look that resembles a hand when viewed from above. Hike the Papase Trail, search for bald eagles in the area, and visit French River Park.

Best times to go:
Spring, Summer, Fall

"THE NEW NORTH"

THE NORTHWEST TERRITORIES

EST. JULY 15, 1870

FACTS ABOUT THE PROVINCE

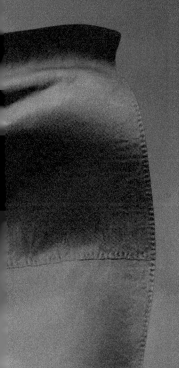

The Northwest Territories of Canada include the regions of Dehcho, North Slave, Sahtu, South Slave and Inuvik. Their remote landscape encompasses forests, mountains, Arctic tundra and islands in the Canadian Arctic Archipelago.

Dehcho's Nahanni National Park Reserve centers around the canyons of the South Nahanni River and 90-meter high Virginia Falls.

The regional capital, Yellowknife, is on the north shore of the Great Slave Lake, with possible views of the northern lights in fall and winter. Exhibits at the Prince of Wales Northern Heritage Centre, by Frame Lake near downtown, highlight the area's human and natural history. The Ingraham Trail, a scenic drive, crosses the Yellowknife River and heads east to lakes and trails.

FAMOUS PERSON BORN IN THE NORTHWEST TERRITORIES

MARGOT KIDDER - ACTRESS

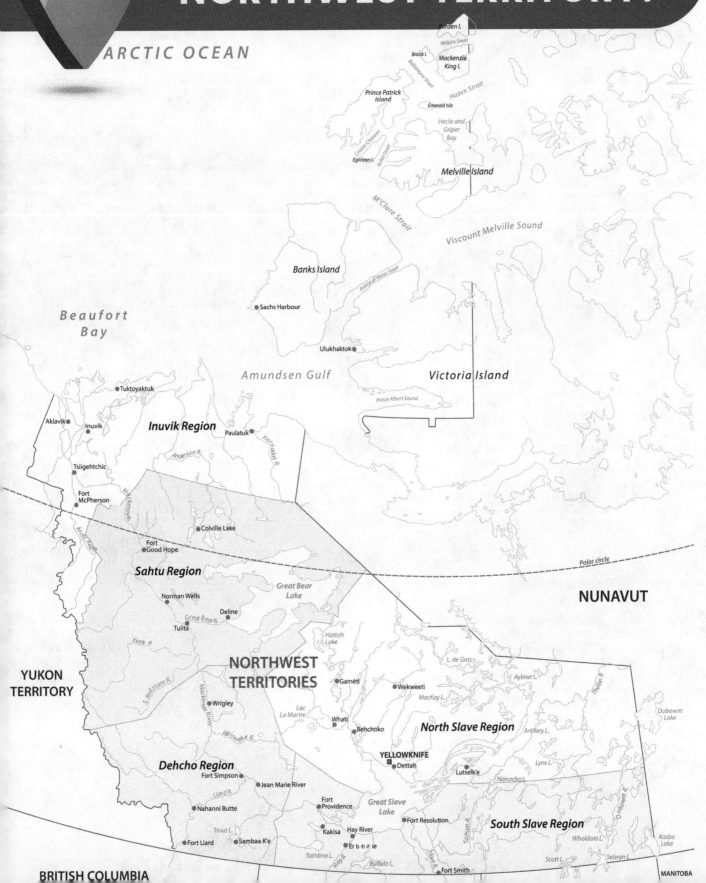

WHERE IN CANADA IS NORTHWEST TERRITORY?

ARCTIC OCEAN

Borden I.
Wilkins Strait
Brock I.
Mackenzie King I.
Ballantyne Strait
Hazen Strait
Prince Patrick Island
Emerald Isle
Hecla and Griper Bay
Crozier Channel
Kellet Strait
Eglinton I.
Melville Island

M'Clure Strait

Viscount Melville Sound

Banks Island
Prince of Wales Strait

Sachs Harbour

Beaufort Bay

Ulukhaktok

Amundsen Gulf

Victoria Island

Prince Albert Sound

Tuktoyaktuk

Aklavik
Inuvik
Inuvik Region
Paulatuk
Anderson R.
Horton R.

Tsiigehtchic
Fort McPherson
Arctic Red R.
Mackenzie R.
Colville Lake
Fort Good Hope

Polar circle

Sahtu Region

Great Bear Lake

NUNAVUT

Norman Wells
Deline
Great Bear R.
Tulita
Keele R.
Hottah Lake
L. de Gras

NORTHWEST TERRITORIES
Gamètì
Wekweeti
MacKay L.
Aylmer L.

YUKON TERRITORY
S. Redstone R.
Wrigley
Mackenzie River
Lac La Martre
Whatì
Behchoko
North Slave Region
Artillery L.
Lynx L.
Dubawnt Lake

Willowlake R.

YELLOWKNIFE
Dettah
Lutselk'e
Nonacho L.

Dehcho Region
Fort Simpson
Jean Marie River
Liard R.
Fort Providence
Great Slave Lake
Fort Resolution
South Slave Region
Wholdaia L.
Kasba Lake

Nahanni Butte
Trout L.
Kakisa
Hay River
Taltson R.
Slave R.
Dubawnt R.
Thelon R.
Scott L.
Selwyn L.

Fort Liard
Sambaa K'e
Tathlina L.
Hay R.
Enterprise
Buffalo L.
Fort Smith

BRITISH COLUMBIA
MANITOBA

VIRGINIA FALLS

Located in the Nahanni National Park Reserve, Virginia Falls is a massive waterfall near the Yukon. Known for being twice as tall as Niagara Falls at 96 m, it's home to a portage trail as well as fossils that are about 300 million years old. The Sluicebox Rapids are also part of the falls. Together with the river below, they are the primary reason why the area is so popular among thrill-seekers who try to navigate their way along the choppy water.

Best times to go:
Spring, Summer, Fall

A herd of Muskox grazing on the grass along the Thomsen River, Aulavik National Park, Northwest Territories

AULAVIK NATIONAL PARK

Located on Banks Island, Aulavik National Park is home to more muskoxen than any other national park in the world. The park has no trees, but it does have Arctic hares roaming free, more than 120 species of flowering plants, and whales in the water. In addition, peregrine falcons, lemmings, snowy owls, and rough-legged hawks are abundant in the area. Take a riveting hike through the tundra, paddle a canoe across the Thomsen River, and bring your binoculars for an unforgettable bird-watching experience.

Best times to go:
Spring, Summer

NAHANNI NATIONAL PARK RESERVE

Located roughly 310 miles to the west of Yellowknife in the Northwest Territories, Nahanni National Park Reserve is a UNESCO World Heritage Site with deep canyons, charming ponds, and a whole lot more. Mount Nirvana, which measures more than 9,000 feet tall, is the park's highest peak. Visit the dramatic Virginia Falls, tromp through Nahanni National Park Reserve's deep forests, and see if you can find the famous short-eared owl!

Best times to go:
Spring, Summer, Fall

GREAT SLAVE LAKE

Located in the southern region of the Northwestern Territories near the border of Alberta, Great Slave Lake is the deepest lake in North America. You can find beautiful beaches enveloping the lake's northern arm, and the eastern arm is famous for its red cliffs. Camp at Thaidene Nene National Park Reserve, go sailing on a breezy afternoon, tour historic Fort Resolution, and visit the large Mackenzie Bison Sanctuary on Highway 3!

Best times to go:
Spring, Summer

MACKENZIE RIVER

Flowing through remote forests and tundra regions of the Northwest Territories, the Mackenzie River has a drainage basin that is second only to the mighty Mississippi River in size. In the 1800s, several points along the river became lucrative business hubs for fur traders. Grab a paddleboat to spend time out on the calmer portions of the water, visit the hot springs, and look for the northern lights whenever they are active!

Best times to go:
Spring, Summer

The Mackenzie River, Northwest Territories

YELLOWKNIFE

Located on the shores of the Great Slave Lake, Yellowknife is the capital of the Northwest Territories. It is also the only city in the region. While some parts of Yellowknife's landscape feature gently rolling hills, other parts are rocky, jagged, and filled with trees. Visit Cameron Falls in Hidden Lake Territorial Park, spend a morning at the Prince of Wales Northern Heritage Centre, and participate in a workshop at the Northern Arts and Cultural Centre. If you are visiting Yellowknife in March, then save a few hours on your itinerary to stop in at Snowking's Winter Festival!

Best times to go:
Spring, Summer, Winter

Tepees with Aurora Borealis at Yellow Knife, Northwest Territories

KAKISA RIVER

Flowing westwards into the Northwest Territories from Alberta and back again, the Kakisa River is one of the famous Mackenzie River's largest tributaries. Kakisa River Territorial Park, which is located just off of Highway 1, is a favorite spot for locals who love to fish. Have a picnic feast outdoors in surrounding woodlands, spend a calm afternoon on a boat tour, and hike to your heart's content through Kakisa Day Use Area.

Best times to go:
Summer, Fall

Quiet evening on the Kakisa River

ALEXANDRA FALLS

The third-tallest falls in the Northwest Territories, Alexandra Falls is one of two major waterfalls featured at Twin Falls Gorge Territorial Park. Amazingly, several outdoor adventurers have actually made successful trips over the falls in kayaks. The park that surrounds the falls features gorgeous campgrounds, hiking trails, and much more. Traverse the boardwalk around the nearby Hay River, climb the spiral staircase next to the falls to get an upfront view, and see how many tree species you can spot in the deep, dense forests of the surrounding park!

Best times to go:
Spring, Summer

Alexandra Falls, Northwest Terrotories

LADY EVELYN FALLS

Located close to Kakisa, a small village in the South Slave Region of the Northwest Territories, Lady Evelyn Falls is one of the major attractions on what is known as "Waterfall Highway" among the locals. Lady Evelyn Falls Territorial Park, which features powered campsites and world-class fishing, is easily accessible by car off of the famous Mackenzie Highway. Gather around a campfire while you spend a night under the stars, cook fresh fish at one of the cooking sites on the grounds, or rent an RV if you'd like to have an extended stay!

Best times to go:
Spring, Summer, Fall

Lady Evelyn Falls, Northwest Territories

Louise Falls in the Twin Falls Gorge Territorial Park, Northwest Territories

LOUISE FALLS

Located in Twin Falls Gorge Territorial Park in the Northwest Territories, Louise Falls is a waterfall on the Hay River. Known as the sister to Alexandra Falls, this stunning wilderness area is easily accessible and breathtakingly beautiful. You can see the falls from the day-use areas of the park. Take a short hike to get closer. The path to Louise Falls culminates in a dramatic spiral staircase.

Best times to go:
Summer

DEMPSTER HIGHWAY

Located in the Northwest Territories, the Dempster Highway is the northernmost road in Canada. Known for being the road to the Arctic Ocean, the entire length of highway has a gravel surface that is up to 2 meters deep to protect the permafrost beneath it. For most of its route, the highway passes no other roads, houses or power lines. Taking a road trip from Dawson City to Inuvik takes at least two days. From Inuvik, you can continue driving to Tuktoyaktuk, a town that was only accessible by air, boat or ice road until the highway was extended in 2017.

Best times to go:
Summer

Our Lady of Victory, Igloo Church, Inuvik, Northwest Territories

IGLOO CHURCH INUVIK

Located along the Mackenzie Delta in the remote Northwest Territories, the Canadian government created Inuvik as a regional center in the 1950s. The Igloo Church, a Catholic parish more properly known as Our Lady of Victory Church, is the only building in Inuvik not built on pilings. It is the best-known building in town, and its domed structure, interior wood buttresses and curved pews provide a unique experience. Masses are held Sundays and on afternoons between Tuesday and Friday.

Best times to go:
Summer

INGRAHAM TRAIL

Located in the Northwest Territories, Ingraham Trail, or Highway 4, is a remote portion of the National Highway System in Canada. Known as a prime viewing location for the northern lights, Ingraham Trail traverses three territorial parks, which offer camping, adventure and a respite from the everyday. Locals call this "cottage country" for its many rental cabins. The trail connects more than 12 lakes, which offer recreational opportunities throughout the year. The hike to the abandoned gold mines near Hidden Lake is especially unique.

Best times to go:
All Year

Igloo, Blachford Lake, Northwest Territories

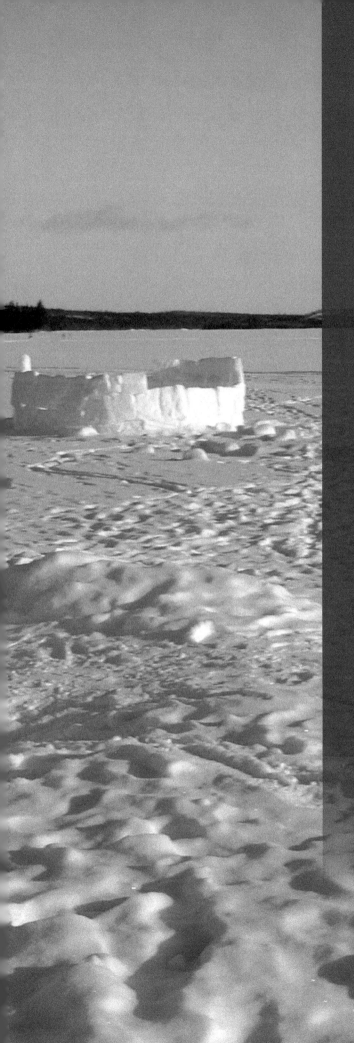

BLACHFORD LAKE

Located near Yellowknife in the Northwest Territories, Blachford Lake is a 7 km wilderness area. The only lodge on the lake is accessible by airplane. Once you arrive, you have full access to nature. Known for being an ideal place to see the aurora borealis, Blachford Lake is incredibly remote. During the winter, you can go snowmobiling, cross-country skiing, snowshoeing, or ice fishing. During the summer months, visitors hike, kayak, and canoe. When you're not adventuring, you can relax in the hot tub at the lodge.

Best times to go:
All Year

CANADA IN PICTURES

COLLECTIONS

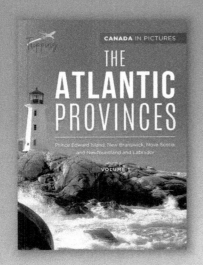

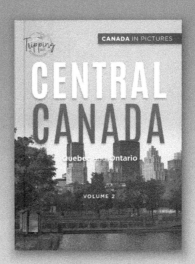

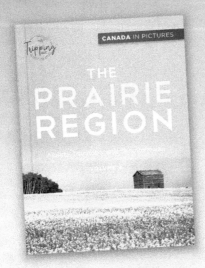

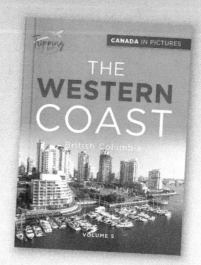

WWW.CANADAINPICTURES.CA

Printed in the USA
CPSIA information can be obtained
at www.ICGtesting.com
LVHW080242211023
761656LV00065B/1020

9 780228 236221